The Hull with It

The Hull with It

a memoir

You Can Go Home Again

Susan Eastman

Annotation Press (a division of WinePress Publishing, PO Box 428, Enumclaw, WA 98022) functions only as book publisher. As such, the ultimate design, content, editorial accuracy, and views expressed or implied in this work are those of the author.

ISBN 13: 978-1-59977-032-1
ISBN 10: 1-59977-032-6
Library of Congress Catalog Card Number: 2011929815

To my dad

Contents

Acknowledgments

THIS STORY ACKNOWLEDGES all you Hullians wherever you may be today.

I would like to thank all my childhood friends who have helped me keep these wonderful memories of you alive. Thanks to the ones I have reconnected with, the others whom I remember fondly, and those I have met through the years when visiting on vacation. Thanks to those strangers whom I have encountered on the beach, in a local restaurant, or even walking along a road. You all have made me a happier person when I hear of your love for this magical place called Nantasket Beach.

To my husband, Ray, if you had not encouraged me I would never have attempted to put my ideas down on paper.

Prologue

AS I TURNED the bend of the road into the serenity of Nantasket Beach, I was home again.

In the summer of 1989, I anticipated my first return to my childhood surroundings with my husband and stepson. In my head, I had pictured how we would all react and feel about this day. I was happily surprised to have such an exciting reaction from my husband and my stepson. And with a picture perfect, sunny day, nothing could have been more special—never knowing what would come of the day or how the future would change after that day.

Not realizing what impact my childhood would mean to me many years later to be going home and to be moving through the past. What an impact that this small town of Hull had made on my life, and how the children I had met during the years when I lived there would stay in my heart and memory fifty years later.

Chapter 1

City Living

IN 1952, WHEN I was six years old and my brother Neal was two, we were living in Boston in a three-story apartment building. The way neighborhood children cooled off on hot, humid summer days was to stand in front of open fire hydrants and let the water spray us or sometimes run through the spray as though it was like a lawn sprinkler. That was something we would look forward to and it would be our entertainment for the day.

We lived across the street from the Franklin Park Zoo in the suburb of Roxbury. I remember that on Sundays my parents would take my brother and me to the zoo. It was always a great treat for us children and a low-cost day's outing for my parents. On other

Sundays we were likely to be watching a Red Sox baseball game—or I should say my parents would be. I can remember my mother, in order to get a little peace and quiet, would get into my little brother's playpen and watch the game from there while my dad kept an eye on my brother and me.

There were places we could go to that were within walking distance and, if there were not, another option was the streetcar just across the street from where we lived. It was not easy to have a day's outing without a family car of which we did not own at that time. It couldn't have been easy for my mother either when living on the third floor as she would have to lug a baby carriage and all the necessities for the day down and up again with two children in tow.

Chapter 2

Visits to the Beach

MY DAD'S PARENTS had a year-round home at Nantasket Beach in Hull, Massachusetts. I remember my grandfather coming to the city to pick up the family on a Sunday to take us to the beach. We would drive back the same night. As you will read later on, that really was quite a sacrifice for him considering how much distance and time it took. The times that we went to and from the beach on the same day were a very big treat for all of us.

Having Dad's family living at Nantasket Beach gave him an extra pull to want to see his family move there someday. Until it was possible for my parents to buy a home, my dad saw to it that his family would be able to stay at Nantasket Beach for at least a month during the summer, and he would come down on weekends by commuter boat. He would come on a Friday night after spending the workdays in the hot city. My dad was a very devoted father and was always thinking of his family's needs.

In the same respect, his love of his parents never ended. In later years, I can remember all of us sitting around the table after dinner. Every night my dad would call his mother and talk for at least an hour. Some might call him a mama's boy, which he probably was, but nonetheless, he was a wonderful husband and father as well.

When we spent time at the beach, we would rent one of the rooms on the second floor of a large home. All four of us stayed in that one room. We had kitchen privileges. It could be very warm in our room as our windows faced the street and not the ocean. The house was located just one block from the beach. It was very convenient for the family to walk over with all the paraphernalia needed for the children to play at the beach.

At this time my brother Neal was only a baby, was not a very good sleeper, and would cry nonstop at night. So as not to disturb the other family members in the house my dad would drive him around in the car to lull him to sleep.

My dad and brother

Me at age six years

Chapter 3

Move to the Beach

IT WAS VERY exciting when we moved to our first home in the beautiful small beach community of Nantasket Beach, where we would live year-round. We were living on a brand-new street where very few homes had been built at the time. The roads had not even been paved on our street, so it was almost like a continuation of the beach with sand everywhere, just like a large sandbox.

All the young families were beginning to move in with their children of various ages. This gave us a chance to size up the ages of the children and get to know them separately before the next family moved in.

For me, being in a beach town named Hull, Massachusetts, was magical. Added to this, we were living only seven blocks from the ocean, which made the whole experience even more special. The long sandy beach stretched on for as far as the eye could see. It was made of beautiful, fine, light gray sand. The azure water and gentle waves lapped at the sand. At that time there was an amusement park that went on for blocks and blocks. It was located right at the entrance to the town. It helped lure people to make the drive from the city on a hot summer day.

The drive in the fifties was torturous. The traffic would be bumper to bumper on the weekends all summer long. I don't think things have changed that much as far as the roads and the number of people who still make the trip down to the beach. Road construction hasn't improved much in almost fifty years.

Most of the areas on the beach sand where you could lie on a blanket or sit on chairs were covered by the ocean at high tide, and everyone would be pushed up to a sea wall at such times. The wall came in handy when we were running to get ice cream from the ice cream truck because you could cool off your feet while waiting your turn by sitting on the wall and letting your hot feet dangle. The sand was so hot it could burn your skin off. In those days we never put on shoes for that run, we just did it.

At low tide you would have to walk forever to the water, and once you reached the water there were sandbars. It was a long process of finally getting wet. Between the beach and the ocean, there were shallow tide pools of still, warm water. At the time, we were not aware that it might be stagnant water with diseases festering in it. Little children sat in the warm water. The mothers were with them, either parked in their chairs in the water, or just sitting directly in the warm water with the children.

One year in the fifties there was a terrible outbreak of polio, and some attributed it to the stagnant water and the elements that were present in the stagnant water. It hit many people in our town and I can remember hearing about the iron lungs that were distributed to different homes. At least one resident had a pool installed in his backyard so that his wife could exercise and possibly recover from this dreadful disease.

The night before the polio outbreak was publicized in the news, we were visiting my aunt and uncle and their children who also lived at the beach. As always, we would kiss everyone when we arrived and then again when we left. Well, the next morning after we had kissed everyone goodbye, my aunt called to tell us that my cousin had come down with a very mild case of polio. She advised us all to get shots. Luckily the doctors in our town had the medication on hand. We were all fine, never having any signs of the disease at all, and my cousin, who did come down with a light case, recovered and was just fine.

Chapter 4

Nostalgia

EVEN TODAY, SO many years later, when my husband and I go back there, Nantasket Beach has that same magical feeling. When we turn the bend coming into town and I have my first look at the sparkling blue ocean with the sun glistening upon the waves, I have the same feeling I had as a child. We are back. I am back home again.

Chapter 5

The Peninsula

NANTASKET BEACH, IN particular, is made up of glacial soils that have been reworked into a remarkable beach of fine, light gray to light brown sand with occasional windrows of gravel and cobbles. Nantasket means "place of low tide" and was so named many years ago due to the many acres of tidal flats exposed around the harbor area. Nantasket Beach itself is related to a large north-south trending sandbar or peninsula of some half-mile wide by three miles long. At its southerly end, the beach is anchored to the mainland's ancient bedrock of some six hundred million years in age. Otherwise it is related to much younger glacial detritus of some twenty thousand years in age. The glacial soils, in turn, are made up by an admixture of silts, clays, sands, gravel, and cobbles of various colors and bedrock types. Nantasket Beach proper, of course, lies near sea level. Topographic features of interest along the harbor side include several hills of glacial detritus that stand out and are known as "drumlins."[1]

SKETCH MAP FOR A PORTION OF HULL

[1] Acknowledgments to my husband the geologist for this insightful synopsis.

Chapter 6

Friendships

MY FIRST BEST friend was Debby, who lived on the next street to us. As everyone began to move in, there were more children to get to know, and every day was an adventure. As we didn't have fences separating the homes at the beginning, we were able to walk freely here and there, and we went from one yard to the other. I don't quite remember when, but at some point I wandered over to Debby's area, and that started our relationship. A first friend relationship—as we now know—is one of the most impressionable friendships, and has a lot to do with how our other relationships will develop in the future.

Debby's brother and my brother had a very memorable first meeting. My brother was only three and he was always mischievous. The two of them had a fight. Afterward, my brother Neal came home with blood running out of the top of his head. We tried to console my mother—something that we both continued to do throughout her life. Neal wanted to reassure her that he was fine. He really was fine. It looked worse than it really was. I don't remember the boys ever playing together again.

Being as this was a new neighborhood with only three or four homes, the streets were not paved as yet. The roads as such still consisted of sand, which didn't seem to matter that much as there was very little traffic and it gave us children a local place to put up a few tents. They consisted of old blankets and sticks—a makeshift setup. Our tents would remain standing for a while, and we were able to play in them day after day. To us they were our treehouse's on the ground. A place of our own. We would meet there and make plans for the day.

Every house that went up on the street was a house my mother was able to sell. In those days you didn't have to have a real estate license. She just worked with a local builder who lived a few streets away. It was never a nine-to-five job that would keep her away from her family. She seemed to work when my dad was at home, either at night or a few hours on the weekend. This gave her extra money she could use to buy things for our home or use for entertaining, which she loved to do as elegantly as possible.

We were never inside in the summer. From morning to night there seemed to always be so much to keep us busy. We often climbed Strawberry Hill, an easily accessible small hill, just a few streets away. At the time the hill seemed a huge chore for us to conquer, and it would take us most of the morning to accomplish the climb. There was, and still is, a water tower at the top that is a landmark of the town. Now there are houses on Strawberry Hill, and I doubt if little children climb the hill anymore.

I remember in the summer after a long day at the beach, we would come home on Friday nights and go to children's services at the community center—an extension of the Temple. After getting all cleaned up from a day at the beach and putting on something special, we would go to the community center that was just a few streets away. For this occasion, they would have a simple service with prayers and a lot of singing of Jewish songs geared toward the young children. Afterward there was a social hour and snacks. This would be another way to meet children in the area as everyone was welcome.

In the wintertime we would occupy another portion of the community center as an after-school place to meet and do crafts. There were many activities to keep us busy. This would give the children a good place to go when they were housebound because of the snow or as a drop-off place on the way home from school. I don't mean that the parents would drop us off like they do today. We would either get off the bus from school or walk over there on our way home from school. There would always be an instructor there to help with a project of one sort or another. In the beginning, we even had our brownie scout meetings there until our leader started having them in her home.

One winter my folks offered me a chance to take ballet and tap lessons. I was so excited to be going with one of my friends who happened to be the most popular and prettiest girl in the crowd, and who had, even at the young age of eleven, all the boys chasing her. We went to a very small building quite close to the house. I brought my tap shoes and ballet slippers, anticipating how much fun this would be. It was a very frustrating afternoon, which left me wondering what I was doing there.

I couldn't succeed in catching on, so my parents took me out of the class. I just went and observed my friend Susan, and when her father took her to Boston for lessons, I went and watched in admiration. Perhaps it was because her mother had been a dancer that she too possessed the talent. Thinking that helped me rationalize Susan's talent anyway.

Seeing as we were all new to the town, we became great friends, especially those within a three-street radius. There were a few boys in the group, but the majority were girls.

We would play outside as much as possible and have our hopscotch and jump rope games ongoing in the street day after day. We never seemed to fight, but I do remember one of the girls was a few years younger than the rest of us, and at this young age, it seemed to matter. The other children would hide from her, which, of course, was very cruel. I befriended her. I always chose to go with the underdog. She turned out to become a very good friend, and eventually the other girls accepted her.

As the summer progressed, there were many more people moving to the beach and more friends for us to get to know. After dinner, we would gather in one of our backyards, and I can remember one time playing spin the bottle. Today our innocence would be laughed at, but we thought we were very grown up. How times have changed.

My friend Debby

My friend Susan

My friends Susan and Debby

Chapter 7

Summer Fun

NANTASKET BEACH WAS and still is a most beautiful beach. There are "miles and miles" of white sand and beautiful gentle waves most of the time. When there are storms the beach can be dangerous, and as at other beaches, drownings have occurred. One time we had to be evacuated during a severe storm on the bayside where we lived. I can remember boats coming for us after the water went over a small wall that was located there.

We always walked to the beach as we were just a few streets away. At that time it seemed very far for our children's legs, but today walking to the beach seems like nothing. On the way to the beach we would pick up each person as we passed his or her house. Those who were not on our way would meet us at the beach. If the sun was shining the beach was where we would be, and we always sat at the end of our special street at the beach—Colburn Avenue.

There was no need for parents to watch us as there were lifeguards. Those were different times. It was so much safer, and we kids would usually stay in a group. When the mothers came down, they did not sit by us. They didn't want to embarrass us. I am sure they kept an eye on us being as we all sat within earshot of each other.

When we went into the water, we all went together and usually stayed for hours. It took a while to get in. The water was like ice and you would have to first numb your ankles by standing in the water. Then slowly you would go all the way down in the water until you were so numb you felt nothing. After that process, who would want to get out and start over again? However, it was so refreshing after having the hot sun beating on you that we went in often. We were allowed to have inner tubes, and that was the best way for us to stay out in the water and just ride over the gentle waves. We could still socialize as we bobbed up and down.

Sometimes we would be so mesmerized by the fun we were having, and we would be so far out, that the lifeguards would wave us in. However, we mostly ignored them. That's about as rebellious as we got. We would finally renege and come in.

On the other end of our street, there was a bay that was very rocky where we could climb and explore new things. If the ocean had jellyfish or an undertow, we walked to the rocky bay instead of the beach. We were so lucky that there was always a place to cool off. You could swim in the bay, but you would have to wear sneakers since sand was almost nonexistent. There were so many boulders and shells that could cut your feet after you got out that it really wasn't a place to lie on the beach. We were children, so we made the best of it.

We all had bikes. They were nothing special, but they were our transportation. We could get anywhere on our bikes, and were able to ride on the back roads as they would be almost car free. As we liked to ride three across, that was a good thing.

In the morning we would ride up to Kenberma Street, where all the kids would be hanging out, and usually meet some new kids, and plan to meet them on the beach later.

There were different stores up there, and one or two of us would usually have to pick something up at the store or Weinberg's Bakery for our mothers. We liked going into the corner store named Huskins, where we played the pinball machine till our money ran out. I still love playing pinball machines to this day. There was also a penny candy store that was a great treat, and it would take us forever to pick out just the right candies. There also was a post office at this corner where you would pick up your mail. So this area was, and still is, the hub at this end of town.

When we came back from Kenberma Street, more often than not we would play canasta at one of the children's homes. We never got bored with it. I'm happy that I learned the game at a young age. I still play it and love being in a canasta group today.

After lunch we would go to the beach for the rest of the day. It was "miles and miles" of sand and the group would walk and walk, wanting to be noticed. Each cliqué sat at a different street at the beach. We thought our area was very popular. We would gather some new kids and have them come to sit with us on the sand for hours till it got too cool to sit there anymore. Sometimes we stayed after it was too cool. Occasionally, we would meet our friends after dinner at the beach where we would watch the fireworks from Paragon Amusement Park that went off every night.

My friend Debby's father drove an ice cream truck in the summer, and believe me, he was the most popular dad. The ice cream trucks would come by the beach every hour. Our mothers only allowed us one ice cream a day. That was tough. Once a week, though, we were allowed a special ice cream from the truck. This one treat would be twice as expensive as everything else on the truck. Somehow, that one tasted more special, and we always looked forward to it. If we happened to be at Debby's house at night when her father pulled up with his ice cream truck, all the kids were given ice cream at no cost. How lucky were we?

We even had some romances, even though we were no older than ten. Mostly we would all be friends, boys and girls, but then there were the summer kids who would infiltrate our group and that changed everything. One family of summer residents on the street where I lived had a son who was a little younger than us and cute as can be. Well, all of the girls were falling all over him. He decided if he kissed you, you would be going steady with him. So for two weeks out of the summer he gave you his ID bracelet and he would be your boyfriend for those two weeks, and you would go everywhere with him holding hands. After that he would move on to another girl. Sometimes he was on a second round and you got to go steady with him again before he had to go back to the city.

Chapter 8

Paragon Park

ONE OF THE mainstays of the town was Paragon Amusement Park, where people would come from different towns to spend a day at the beach and enjoy the park. The park took up a large portion of the area where you drive into the town, and it sat across the street from the ocean. When you came around that bend into town you would feel the road vibrate from the motion of the wooden roller coaster, and you could actually hear the clickety-clack of the roller coaster on the track. From everywhere in the park, you could hear the screams of the roller coaster riders. The park had everything one could imagine: circus acts and all kinds of amusements—and food. You could eat anything you wanted from cotton candy, big balls of colored popcorn, pizza, and hotdogs. The best fried clams that you could ever buy came in a box from which you could just walk around and eat to your heart's content.

Even as you came around the bend into the town, you could smell all the aromas emanating from the park. That aroma of all the wonderful things meant to me being a child. All the typical rides were there. A couple rides I loved were the whip and the caterpillar. There were the usual games you could try to win stuffed animals. Skeet ball was my favorite, and I could be there for hours trying to win tickets that gave you a silly prize that you could have bought for half the price. We all knew the truth, but didn't care.

Once a summer my folks would take my brother and me to Paragon Park on a spending spree of twenty-five dollars. When that money ran out we had to go home. It really was something we looked forward to. It was such fun, mainly because we were all together. I do not think we were ever there more than a few hours. Can you imagine the kids of today being satisfied with that? Of course, this was in the fifties.

When we got a little older, a group of us would go to Paragon Park without our parents. I believe the park was only open in the summer because of the weather and, of course, all the rides were out in the open. There was also a roller skating rink in the park. It was a place that we could get into trouble if we were not careful as a few times we would go there and pick up boys.

The park, as I said before, was really the only other draw at that time besides the beautiful beach that would bring people into the town. They would have all the food stands and the carnies who would be yelling at people to play and win a prize. Lots of people would throw money into a game and never realize that most of the time it was fixed. Very few people won. I knew this at a young age because an uncle of mine worked there on the weekends. If I was down at the park and saw him, I would play and I always won.

Chapter 9

The Surf Club

AROUND THE TIME I was ten, my friends and I were allowed to walk all the way to the other end of town at night to go to a kids' nightclub called "The Surf." It served no alcohol, just Cokes. We were always there early so we could have a dance spot up front. The girls would dance with girls as our group usually only had one or two boys. They would have Arnie Ginsberg as the disc jockey at some of the hops. At the time he was one of the most popular disc jockeys in Boston. The groups that performed there were always the most popular at the time: Bobby Riddell, Fabian, and so many of the others. So many of the singers were just beginning. How lucky we were to have this available to us in this small town. After the show was over, we would walk home together and not have to worry about our safety.

Chapter 10

Family Times

IN THIS SMALL beach town, there were quite a few family members who lived just streets away. It was wonderful for me because I could ride my bike to my grandparents' house. I took the back streets with beautiful trees that would shade my way. In the summer it would get very hot. I would have a short visit with my grandparents and with any cousins who might also be there.

There were always barbecues on weekends in my grandparents' beautiful backyard. At least part of the family would be there for a day's visit every weekend. All but one of my dad's siblings and families lived there, so there was always an opportunity to visit with cousins and have someone to play with who was our own age.

One aunt and uncle had a house built right next door to my grandparents. Almost like the show *Everybody Loves Raymond,* there was quite a bit of visiting back and forth, and also a lot of tension that went on.

My aunt was one of the sweetest people and always wanted to please her parents and her family. She was not a well person, and I'm sure was mostly glad to have her parents close by to help with the children. Her husband, my uncle, was a gem of a husband. He helped my aunt as much as he could, but also had to be on the road with his job. Having three out of four children living in the same small town surely had to be very satisfying for my grandparents.

One of my grandfather's hobbies was tending to his garden. The flowers and the lawn were always perfectly manicured. His yard was even featured in a *Home and Garden* magazine.

Before or after the barbecue, we would all walk down to the beach and have a family day at the ocean. This was probably also to let the grandchildren run to their heart's content and to give the parents some alone time.

There was also the downside of being in a small town and having your extended family around to tease you and really to know your every move. My first kiss experience was one of those experiences that was not only told to my best friend over the phone, but also to my grandmother, who was eavesdropping on the extension phone. She related to me afterward that, "Oh, he was a real man I kissed." He was probably just a few years older than me, but at the time it seemed so special and she just loved to embarrass me as often as she got the chance.

That time in my life is when my roots were planted. As I've moved through my life, I've never forgotten about this time, and I have added layers to my early experiences. Just as an onion has layers starting deep inside and adds more as time passes, so I have begun with my early experiences in Nantasket and have added layers to my life. I am continuing up the path from where I came. I feel so fortunate to have been born when I was. Looking back, I can see how simple things were then, and I can see that this generation seemed to appreciate everything.

Having siblings gives you another layer through which to connect and grow. Even more than your parents, they can know your heart and soul more than anyone else. They may not always remember things the same way you did, but their story can be added to your story. Lucky for me, I have that relationship with my brother Neal. Now that Mom and Dad are gone and we have only each other from our immediate family left, I now can appreciate what I heard from my mother for years when she said, "You just have each other, so always be close."

Chapter 11

Long Summer

As CHILDREN, WE always looked forward to summer. To me it was the beginning of the year. It was almost like a fresh start with a new beginning. So the last day of school was quite a joyous time in that we could be free of all commitments and look forward to the summer people arriving in a few weeks.

I can remember only one summer that the sun never came out. It rained almost every day. We had one movie theater in Hull, the Apollo and Bayside Theatre. It only opened on rainy days, so that summer must have been a good one for them. When you wanted to go to the theater, you had to call ahead just in case they would not be open even on a rainy day.

We were so bored trying to find things to do while we were inside the house or on the porches keeping out of the rain and downright horrible weather that we could hardly wait to return to school that year. At one point that summer, my friend Debby and I decided to collect all the things we thought we could sell. There was a woman in town whom we called "the gypsy." She had collected all her old costume jewelry and I guess everything else she wanted to sell and put it out on her lawn. It was the first-known garage sale. Getting the idea from her, we set up our own little stand with lemonade and gift items, and ended up making some good spending money.

I also did a lot of babysitting. Sometimes it would be for a complete day while the parents were in Boston. One family owned a clothing business and instead of money, I was able to go down to the basement where they stored their merchandise and pick out outfits with a dollar value that was equivalent to the hours I had babysat. I found that very rewarding. That was a good summer for me, wardrobe wise. I don't think I ever before or since had so many shorts outfits.

Chapter 12

Some Changes

WHEN I WAS a child, we had only one restaurant and one bakery in town, and they were frequented by the families who lived in our end of town. Weinberg's Bakery is still there after sixty years. It is owned by a different family, but the name is the same. Cohen's Deli, however, has gone along with a lot of the families who moved away. It had the best food you could imagine—other than if your grandmother made it.

Really not as much has changed in these many years as one would think. The wonderful Paragon Amusement Park has been gone since 1984. It was replaced by tall brick condominiums that don't even seem to fit the style of a beach town as most of the homes here are wood. The new homes that have been built are open and airy looking.

Luckily, the carousel, the clock tower, and a few of the food stands from the original Paragon Park remain to keep the nostalgia going. The excitement that once was in that part of town, though, has gone. Walking around, I can remember how it was. I know I can feel the ghost of times past when I am there.

There are still inhabitants that have stayed here, or they come back to their family homes for the summer. Much has stayed the same in that Nantasket is still a small town, and the friendliness and the warmth of the people hasn't changed. I always feel welcome and that I am back home again after all these many years.

I didn't realize until many years after I lived in Nantasket Beach that there were different sections of town in which different ethnic groups lived. That's why we had Cohen's Deli and also a Jewish bakery. It was something we didn't think about. It just was. We didn't eat out as much as people do today. We ate out mainly on special occasions such as a Girl Scout meeting, then we would frequent Cohen's Deli. It was the place to go. In the summer, all of the grandchildren worked in this family-owned restaurant. Other family members who were schoolteachers with the summer off also worked there. When eating in the restaurant you really had to be on your best behavior as you might be waited on by your next year's schoolteacher. As this was a very small town they would remember you. The bakery, as I said, is still there and I visit it at least once on each visit that we make back to the beach. It has different family owners, but the name and the building are still there.

In those days my grandfather would walk up to the bakery every morning and get fresh bread and baked goods for the day. That was an incentive for me to drop by my grandparents in the morning. I knew there would always be something yummy to eat.

Chapter 13

My Grandparents

MY DAD'S PARENTS didn't seem as important in my early life as they do now. I have now had time to think about the dynamics of our family and what really pulled it together—having grandparents who gave of their time and love, and having them living at such close proximity made me feel loved. That is exactly what a family unit should be all about. It was a simple time in the fifties, yet things were far from perfect. To me the simplicity of it is what seems to be missing from our everyday life today.

By the time the grandchildren started coming, my grandparents had a small but beautiful home in Nantasket Beach that was just streets from the beach.

My grandmother had every luxury she desired. My grandfather was very good to her. In the winter they would go to Florida and stay at the Fontainebleau Hotel.

I don't know about the other grandchildren, but during the time my grandparents were in Florida, my brother and I were required to write a letter every week and tell our grandparents about the goings on in our life. My grandfather would reply to these letters, as my grandmother did not learn to read or write till very late in her life. My grandparents were immigrants from Russia and were married and had children very young—I think starting at fifteen. My grandfather worked very hard when he came to this country. I'm sure it wasn't easy with four children. My grandmother would have a tutor come to the house to teach her. I can remember her sitting and practicing at the kitchen table. She was very determined to conquer reading and writing. She did eventually.

When my grandparents came home, all of the family was summoned for a visit. At this time we would receive exactly the same present for each of the nine grandchildren. If it was bathing suits, all the girls would get bikinis, and the boys would get swim trunks and shirts to match. Also the daughters and daughters-in-law and sons and sons-in-law would receive exactly the same gifts. That went on for many years till my grandmother was too ill to go to Florida.

When they were at home in Nantasket Beach, my grandfather did most of the cooking and baking. He was way ahead of his time. My grandmother would sleep till noon after a late night of card playing, and by the time she would get up, my grandfather would have lunch ready for her. Don't get me wrong; she was a great cook, but he was too.

We were really spoiled with the best vegetables from my grandparents' garden. Every time the family went over there, which was at least once a week, we would come home with a good supply of vegetables. Also, the canned vegetables and pickles my grandmother made were really special.

My grandfather was a tailor and eventually owned a cleaning establishment that after many years was sold to one of my uncles, his youngest son. Every summer we would give him all our wool clothes and coats and whatever else needed cleaning, and he would clean them at no cost. That had to be quite a large savings for the families.

I also remember that when we would go for a family visit, my grandmother would be waiting for the family to arrive, and no matter who came in she would never move from her lounge chair in the backyard. All of us would go over to her and kiss her when we arrived and when we left. She wasn't old, but she just didn't get involved with the grandchildren as my grandfather did. He was a real hands-on grandparent.

Chapter 14

My Home

MY FAMILY'S HOME was a modest home without a basement. The newer ones were being built with basements. We had three bedrooms, but only one bathroom. That was common in those days. The backside of the house was covered with windows from floor to ceiling that overlooked a nice-sized backyard.

The largest room we had was the living room. It had a brick fireplace that took up one entire wall. This was the only room that was carpeted and the one room that we weren't allowed to walk through. It was meant for company only, and no one else sat in there. I guess that was what made the house seem even smaller to me. It was as if that room wasn't even there. You had to walk all around the perimeter of the house so as not to walk on that carpet. The only time I remember enjoying that room was when my parents would be going out on a Saturday night and my mother would lay her full-length mink coat on the couch. I was then allowed to lie on it while she was getting ready. Strange rules, but that was the way it was, and we didn't question it. When we had company, we would be invited to visit with them for a short while as the expression went that "children were seen but not heard."

My parents had a wonderful circle of friends that they kept all their lives. There were five regular couples who would either come to our house, go to one of the other couples' homes, or would meet at a restaurant on Saturday nights. I always remember my mother making the plans all day Saturday on the phone, and then when my dad got home she directed him as to what would be going on that night. This went on just about every Saturday night.

One of the couples, the only one who wasn't married, came to stay one weekend. (That was pretty risqué in those days.) They came for a very special occasion. My uncle Al, as I called him, was going to propose to one of my parents' lifelong friends. I was given the honor of going into Boston with my uncle Al to help pick out her engagement ring. I felt like such a grownup, and I was so proud as I truly loved Al and was so happy for him. He was the only man who smoked cigars that I could stand to be around.

After picking out a beautiful ring, my uncle Al bought me a necklace with a drop on it. He had a way of making everyone feel special. I couldn't believe how sweet he was, I have kept the stone from the drop as a memory into later years of my life.

It was such a happy time for me, I remember going to sleep and feeling complete contentment and safety even with all three of the windows in my small room open. As a child, you may not have had any idea how simple and innocent life was at that time, but later will reflect on it and long for those days.

We had no air conditioning at all in the home, and at times it could become very close as we lived on the bay side. This was the warmest side and was unlike the ocean side that would normally be a lot cooler with an ocean breeze.

My brother and I each had our own room except for one summer when my folks rented out my brother's room to an elderly couple. My brother and I had to share my room. Well, lucky for us and unlucky for the older couple, their stay didn't last long.

The six of us had to share one bathroom. One morning, after the older lady had stayed a very long time in the bathroom, my mother went to check on her, and found her dead. That was the last of my parents ever renting out a room.

My mom and me

My brother

Chapter 15

Daddy's Girl

WE WERE PUT to bed before my dad got home. Even though I was nine and it was summer and still light outside, it was my parents' time to be alone and have their dinner. I'm sure I was the only kid who went to bed so early, but at the time we didn't question it. I would be in bed with my radio listening to *The Shadow* or *The Lone Ranger* and would not go to sleep till my dad came in to kiss me goodnight. The worst punishment for me would be not being kissed. What can I say? I was a daddy's girl.

Some of the best private times I had with my dad were when we lived at the beach and just the three of us—my brother, my dad, and myself—would be at the beach first thing in the morning, even before there were any footprints in the sand or seagulls about. Later on in the day, the seagulls would almost take over the beach as people fed them.

The early morning was really the most peaceful time of the day. At this time we would pick up seashells and sea glass. My dad really loved the ocean and enjoyed playing with us in the sand and water. This gave my mother some alone time to clean without us around. She would bring lunch down to us since being at the beach with dad was an all-day event when we were there on the weekend and family day.

I remember how mad she would get trying to make this drink called Zarex. It was a type of punch syrup that she mixed with water. She never did get it right. It was either too sweet or not sweet enough. But it was cold and wet, and that was all that mattered to us. Why she kept trying it time after time was a mystery to me.

My brother and I had our first experience with gardening with my dad. He started a climbing rosebush for each of us on the side of the house. We each took care of our own bush, and did the watering and pruning. He gave us a love of gardening that, among other things, reminds me of him today. These little moments to me are what keep our loved ones alive to us. If the stories are passed from one generation to the next, it's almost as if those who have gone are still with us even if only in our memories.

I was never allowed pets because my mother was afraid of animals, but one day my dad came home from the golf course with a large turtle. We made a home for it in the backyard, and it seemed to draw the attention of the neighborhood kids who came to look him over. Not long after we got him, he seemed to be less active than usual, and his head stopped popping out. He eventually stopped eating. I, along with some of the neighborhood friends and my brother, took him down to the bay to put him to rest or see if he would go back into the water. As we said our good-byes, we noticed some rough kids stoning the turtle and there was nothing we could do. I guess this was my first experience with cruel children. That was my last pet till I was a teenager.

Chapter 16

Summer's End

BY THE END of the summer we would see our friends one by one moving back to the city. Some would be back again the next year because they had summer homes, whereas others we would never see again, and that was very sad. Mostly at our age we would lose contact with them.

One of the girls I had met during the summer had a family maid whom they brought with them from the city. When I spent the night I was quite impressed by being served breakfast by the maid. I felt like a princess. I can still see my friend's little brother out on the lawn drinking a can of beer in the morning. He was so thin that his folks gave him a can every day being that was the only way he could put weight on. I'm sure today that would never be tolerated.

After everyone left at the end of summer, it wasn't more than a week or two until school started. Usually we were ready for the change of routine and the change of season. One of the schools we attended was at the very easterly end of the town up on a hill. We would go there by bus since it was too far to walk. I can remember thinking it was a big old yellow house with large windows and a wonderful playground. Many years later when I came back to visit, I tried to recall where it was and felt very frustrated that I couldn't have more of a feel for exactly where it had been. As you will be able to tell, I have remembered a lot considering that we only lived in Hull for about seven years and that was sixty years ago.

Just last summer in 2010 while visiting a local hotel, I mentioned the story of the yellow schoolhouse to a young boy working there, and he was able to solve the mystery for me. The school was the Damon School—it is now gone and the space is occupied by a condominium development that is called Damon Place. And, of course, it is on School Street. Mystery solved. It was fun to drive over there and try to visualize all the children running around the schoolyard, and doing twirls on the bars, and playing jump rope.

I remember the weather getting cold pretty fast as the nights lengthened after the time change. The cold would bring us into the house pretty early. All the mothers would have to do was call our names, and one by one every child would take off running for their homes. My mom had a cowbell, so that distinguished her call from the other mothers. However, all the other mothers had distinct calls, and there never was a mistake about who was being summoned. If we didn't hear our mothers, another kid would and tell us we'd better get home. It seemed like we were all running at the same time.

In the younger grades we would walk to school in the snow or whatever the element. We didn't live close to the school. We would put pants on under our dresses to avoid getting too wet and in order to try to stay warm as sometimes we walked in snow drifts to get to school. It was such a project to remove all this clothing and then put it all back on again before leaving for home. Being away from that kind of weather for so long, I have almost forgotten how much work it really was to get ready to go out in the winter.

There were a few snow days when they would close down the schools. When it happened, it would be such fun for us. That was a wonderful excuse to take the sleds out or go ice-skating or both. Everything was right there as we just had to step out of our house and go a few houses down the street to where the owners had left for the winter. There we would find great slopes in their backyards. The snow would be so high sometimes that we would walk up the hill and sink in up to our knees. We made run after run. It was so much fun for us. Finally our toes, faces, and fingers would feel so numb that we would retreat inside for a while and warm up.

Usually on weekends we would go ice-skating on the pond at the next street—we would put guards on our ice skates and walk from our house to the park where the pond was. We would skate for hours and hours until it got too dark or too cold. It was usually the latter that drove us inside.

Never in the summer, but so many times in the winter on the weekends, we would watch cartoons all morning at home or at a friend's house. As if we hadn't had enough of that, we would sometimes go to the movie theater—a whole day's experience. For quite awhile the only theater was in the next town and we would have to take a bus to get there. Most families had only one car in the family, and it would be used by the fathers to go to work.

So along with my brother, whom I was required to take, and a friend and her sister, we would trudge off for the day's adventure. Taking our siblings was never fun, but that was the only way we got to go. When I say we spent an entire day at the theater, it is no exaggeration. We would sit through many cartoons, and sometimes two shows. The place was packed to the balcony with kids. You would see popcorn flying as the young boys would try to get a girl's attention. Boys will be boys.

When we got out of the theater, it would usually be nighttime, and we would once again trudge through the snow to wait for the bus home. A good day was had by all of us, and our time away gave our mothers some time for themselves.

Not many mothers worked in those days. My job after school was to baby-sit for the children next door as the woman who lived there had to go to work. This was unusual, but necessary as her husband had passed away. At night she would teach elocution lessons for some of the neighborhood children. She would teach us how to walk and sit and speak correctly, and basically just teach us manners.

This at a young age began to give us confidence and, in turn, later on helped us succeed in life in more ways than professionally. For some, confidence is never achieved and that is a puzzle to me. To move around the world on a daily basis requires one to show strength and a savvy of sorts. Today my granddaughter Michelle still gives me the label of Miss Manners. She has learned a lot from me, and realizes how important it is to feel comfortable in all situations. This is something that is really missing today—the loss of manners.

As young as I was, the experience to this day still brings back the happiest memories of a wonderful innocent childhood. We always had fun, we were never bored, and this without gadgets—just our imagination.

Chapter 17

Life-Changing Times

I THOUGHT THAT Nantasket Beach would be where I would live forever. Here was the place to be sheltered and protected. But it was all about to come to an end along with my childhood. If I had stayed until I was an adult, it might not have seemed as magical to me as it does now. I did leave the beach and now I will never know.

When I was thirteen, I was told we were moving. My first reaction was of sadness to be leaving my friends and the surroundings with which I felt most comfortable. The next thought was of excitement for our new adventure.

I came home from school the next afternoon to find the principal of my school in the living room with my mother. I didn't know it at the time, but he was there for my mother to show him the house so he would be able to recommend our home to one of the teachers needing a place to live the following school year.

I was shocked and speechless when he asked me to do the invocation on that Friday in front of the entire school in the auditorium. This was something I could not have imagined myself doing as I was awfully shy. Well, somehow I said yes and there I was on Friday standing in front of the entire school leading everyone in a prayer before we started our day. I was so proud the next day when I saw my name in the newspaper.

There was a small party with my friends to say farewell as we would be moving out of state. I knew I would probably never return to live in the same home again. Our house was sold and the moving truck was coming to pick up all our belongings.

We moved back to New England after a short stay in the south. My dad became ill and had to leave his job. Not knowing all the details at the time, we moved to Florida for a few months for him to recuperate and rest before coming back to New England.

Luckily for us we were able to stay in my dad's sister's furnished basement apartment in Nantasket Beach till my dad was able to return to his old job. Then, when he could work, we moved to Boston and lived in an apartment. It was something I never got use to, and really I always hoped that things would go back to the way they were at the beach—but they never did.

We would go back and visit the beach as many members of our family were still living there. Occasionally I would go and stay with my best friend Debby. But it never seemed the same and I never felt that I fit into the old surroundings anymore.

Not until almost a lifetime later did I realize how very special my friend Debby was to me. She was the first child I met when first moving to Nantasket Beach. I remember spending the weekend at her house a few times. Once when her grandparents were visiting, she and I snuck out and took her grandfather's car and drove it around town in the middle of the night. She had no license and could barely see over the steering wheel. It was lucky for us that we didn't get stopped. There were some other occasions when we did get into trouble. It was all part of growing up and testing the waters—or perhaps it was just stupidity.

Chapter 18

Fulfilling My Dreams

AS A MARRIED woman, I always knew that I wanted to share this magical town with my husband and stepchildren, and later with my grandchildren. I suppose I wanted them to see, smell, and feel some of the things that I still visualized in my memories, and what had made me, me. I did not realize until later in life when I had finally visualized my memories that all the strangers I had encountered during my later years would tell me how wonderful their childhood also was growing up in Nantasket Beach. You can actually go home again.

You could say "as luck would have it," but I don't believe in luck. I think you make things happen with your thoughts or your beliefs. Putting yourself "out there" opens doors to many surprises. I continue to reach out and I am continually amazed at the wonderful experiences that enrich my life.

One night I got a call from a friend whose mother had a home in Martha's Vineyard. She was offering to rent it out for a very reasonable price. However, my husband and I had to decide right then. That was easy. "Let's go," I said as I turned to my husband. He said, "Okay."

At this time we were living in California. Fortunately, we love to travel so this would be a great excuse to go back to the East Coast. I had never made it to Martha's Vineyard when I was living in Boston. This would be my first time to experience it, and it would be even better along with my husband, Ray.

The easiest way to reach Martha's Vineyard is by ferry at Woods Hole. Reservations are required before boarding, and since we would be driving a car we would need a special reservation for the car, seeing as there was just so much room available on the boat. All was good as I made the reservations from California. I was sent the tickets that we would have to show upon arrival. The only problem was that when we got there, I had forgotten the tickets at home. It was late at night, and this was the last ferry till morning. We were devastated. It was lucky for us our reservations were on the computer. They let us go through. It once again reminded me of how trusting I have found New Englanders to be.

It was a fabulous trip. We had the most wonderful stay at this quaint Cape Cod house that was close to everything. One thing I had to get used to was that the owner told us the only thing she requested besides watering her plants was not to lock the windows or doors because they would stick shut. That took a few nights to get used to after being away in California for so long where we have everything locked up at all times. We did as she asked and after a while, it gave us a feeling of being free.

I tried very hard not to rush the moment by thinking of my first visit back to Nantasket Beach since I had been married. On the morning that we were to take the ferry back to the mainland from Martha's Vineyard for the drive up the coast to Nantasket Beach we had a picture-perfect day. We had to catch the ferry rather early, but the sun had already become very warm, and we had a clear blue sky ahead.

We spent the last day of our vacation driving back to my childhood home. Also, my stepson, Ben, would be in Maine on vacation and he planned to meet us on this the last day at Nantasket Beach. I had anticipated this time for so long that it was so special to have the day so perfect. I hoped that my husband and stepson would experience the same feelings that I felt.

We met Ben at the designated place on the beach. The sun was shining on the water, the same smells were in the air, the same sounds of all the children playing on the beach, and the mothers still keeping their distance as teenagers congregated on the sand.

It was breathtaking for me to be standing on the same spot I did as a child, and it was like turning the clock back all those many years. It made me so happy to see the reaction of my family and how much they enjoyed the day as I took them around to where all my family and friends had lived. I relayed some of the stories that came to mind. I really hated to leave, but knew we would be back.

Before we left California, I had contacted one of my old Nantasket neighbors who still lived on the same street as I had. She invited the three of us for lunch. Being with her and her husband brought back memories. Their sons had been early friends, and both of them had tragically died just a few years earlier. Sitting here with the parents, I could see the sons alive, just as they were yesterday. Those were good memories. I tried to focus on that and keep the day uplifting.

I wanted to go into the house where I had lived that was across the street from where we were. Even though many years had gone by, the front of the house didn't look too much different. I could see the three windows in the front where my bedroom had been situated. That really brought back memories. The hydrangeas that were out front made me happy. I now have them growing as best as I can at my home in California. They really like the beach, but I am now just a little too far away from a beach to have really full hydrangeas.

Graciously, the woman we were having lunch with took us over and knocked on the door of the house in which a very grumpy man lived. I asked if we could come in just for a moment and look around my childhood home. He wanted no part of it and said we should come back another time. That was impossible as we were leaving that day to head back to Los Angeles. I was heartbroken. Here I was a grown woman standing in the middle of the driveway crying my eyes out.

When I walked on to the next street, I could see into our backyard. It made me sad to see that the yard was not kept up. It was all overgrown. My parents had taken such pride in the yard.

I have walked by many times since then with my husband, but we still have never gone in. Maybe this is better. Seeing it might ruin the vision I have of a cute, well-decorated home that was fairly new and in perfect condition. So most likely my vision will stay that way.

Chapter 19

Return Visits

WE DID HAVE a few opportunities to spend time at Nantasket Beach with my stepdaughter, who, at the time, was living in Providence, Rhode Island. Another time our granddaughter came with us from California. Both occasions were special times that really completed my dream. Little did I know there was more to come.

My husband and I returned to the area every few years and would stay a few towns over in the town of Scituate at a very nice hotel. But every day we would make the half-hour drive to Nantasket Beach to sit at the street where I would sit as a child. On every visit back to Nantasket Beach, my husband and I would drive around to the different streets where my relatives had lived with their families.

Probably unconsciously, I hoped to see someone I knew doing the same thing and remembering the time many years ago when we lived in this area. That never happened.

On one particular visit, however, there were people outside on the lawn where my grandparents had lived. Not being shy as I had been, we stopped the car and the owner came over to see who we were. I did not expect to learn that these were the people to whom my grandfather had sold the house so many years ago. They had even left his family's monogram, located on the shutters, in respect for him.

A husband, wife, and their teenage children lived there at that time. How exciting to be invited inside and to be able to walk through the house. It was a small place, just two bedrooms and one bathroom.

Things looked almost the same. Very few changes had been made. We went downstairs where they had made a nicely furnished basement apartment for their two sons.

I can remember going down there so often to shower after the beach, and at other times to watch my grandfather do his mending on his sewing machine. At the time it wasn't a finished basement. It was pretty musty and could be very damp in the winter.

One summer my grandmother's niece was coming to visit her from Pittsburgh, and I was summoned to come and keep her company. Our age difference was enormous, but I agreed and we got on famously. She had never been married and I remembered my grandmother setting up blind dates for her almost every night that she was there. My grandmother wanted everyone married. She even got on me at the young age of sixteen. It was too bad that she never lived to see me get married.

I would help her niece get ready and wait up to hear how her date went. We would talk all night and giggle, but luckily no one would hear us as we slept down in a basement apartment. I think she enjoyed her visit, but no marriage proposal came out of it, and I don't remember ever seeing her again.

Chapter 20

The New Hotel

IT WAS QUITE ironic that on one visit back to Nantasket Beach we saw a beautiful hotel being constructed right on the site where my childhood dance club, The Surf, had been located. This had later become The Vogue, but then became so run down that it gave the town a very shabby look.

The new hotel was constructed on the outside to be a replica of an old hotel, the Revere House, that had been there many, many years ago and was frequented by the elite of Boston. I kept track of the construction from California and when it was completed, we planned a vacation. It was such a wonderful treat to be able to stay right in Nantasket Beach, and be able to just walk across the street to the ocean.

This has been where we go every few years for a week to two weeks. My husband and I both love it, and I enjoy being home and meeting so many of the people who come back there for some of the same reasons that I do. I feel so lucky that my husband has the same feelings that I do about this little town where I grew up. Now we are making our own memories.

This has been a wonderful journey—one that seems to keep on going. I always feel warm and happy whenever I am back in Nantasket Beach, and now I feel like I never left.

Chapter 21

Friends Reunited

ON ONE OF our last visits to Nantasket Beach, I started to talk with a woman in the lobby of the hotel. This is how New Englanders are—they talk to everyone. Well, this woman happened to have been a neighbor of my first friend Debby when I lived there. She gave me Debby's brother's number and he in turn gave me the phone number of my earliest friend, Debby. She lives in Florida now, but her siblings live in California. This gave me an opportunity—after fifty years— to be reunited with her at her sister Marilyn's home in Palm Desert, California.

Her sister, Marilyn, was just a baby when I left, so this was a double reunion. It was a great day that ran well into the night when we had dinner with our spouses. When we parted, I knew we would stay connected forever.

The following year would be my sixty-fifth birthday. I had planned and talked about it for a year. It was to be a sleepover pajama party with a small group of friends that I had known for a long time. I did not expect Debby to come from Florida, so I was surprised and flattered when I learned she would be there. Her sister, Marilyn, and she came from Palm Desert to join in my celebration. Earlier in the day my husband, Debby, her sister, her brother (whom I hadn't seen since we were children in Nantasket Beach), and I had lunch together. It was a perfect way to start my birthday. We had come full circle and the love and closeness had not wavered. I still feel a special bond and am glad that it has been renewed.

My birthday gift from Debby was a teddy bear dressed like a frilly little girl. When you squeezed her hand a tape played ". . . the good times, the bad times, that's what friends are for." That says it all. Your good friends of a lifetime who know your heart are always there for you.

Thanks to email and the phone, we can now stay in touch and share this part of our lives with each other.

The Hull with it. You can go home again, if you don't lose your childhood innocence.

The End

CPSIA information can be obtained at www.ICGtesting.com
Printed in the USA
LVOW040424010312

271040LV00001B/5/P